HOW TO
READ
PALMS

by Judith Hipskind

CONTENTS

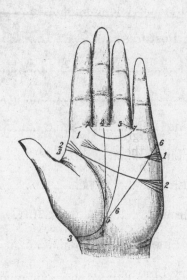

INTRODUCTION

Lift up your hand, spread your fingers and look hard at your palm. The lines, bold and faint, the ridges, the intricate patterns...all of them tell a story that is distinctly your own.

For thousands of years we have been fascinated by the human hand. As early as 3000 B.C. the Chinese called palm reading *siang cheou*. In India the reading of the hand was part of *hast samudrika shastra* – a quasi-science that linked certain physical characteristics to human nature and destiny.

In many minds, of course, palmistry conjures up images of dark-eyed Gypsies, in bright-colored scarves and gold earrings, promising a reading of the future in exchange for a fee. Certainly its close link with the Gypsies is the main reason that palmistry has so often been shrouded in secrecy, intrigue...and suspicion.

No one group has done more to pass on palmistry's secrets than this most mobile and exotic of peoples. As they moved around the world, mixing with all races and cultures, their predictions and insights from the reading of the palms captured people's imaginations – and also inspired more and more curiosity about and investigation of the art.

The Gypsies were perhaps at their most influential during the Middle Ages, when the Holy Roman Empire employed them as part of a far-reaching espionage network. Their mobility made them perfect spies as they moved from town to town, and court to court, listening, watching, and piecing together odd scraps of information to relay back to their masters. The intimacy of a palm reading, of course, was a great opportunity to ask probing questions about what was going on – including changing alliances and military movements.

7

Inevitably, Gypsies became regarded as dangerous people to know, and palmistry itself fell into disrepute.

Of course, Gypsy spies were not alone in misusing palmistry. Rulers, too, wielded it as a tool for political gain and personal fortune. After all, information of any kind was so scarce. Someone who knew how to read hands could at least claim inside knowledge of the future, and thus influence life and death decisions of state.

It's easy to understand, for example, how a slave captured in war had one up on his new master if he could predict his future!

Just imagine a world without CNN and newspapers, no telephones, spreadsheets, financial forecasts, or all that sophisticated trend-predicting technology we have today. Imagine news only by word of mouth – relayed by messengers on foot.

Or imagine living in such a world when your daughter 500 miles away is expecting her first baby. You'd have to wait days for any news of the newborn to reach you – unless someone can tell you some other way that the birth occurred, and that mother and baby are well...

Imagine you know the old king is dying, and when he goes, the life of your city or countryside is going to be turned upside down. How nice to have some way – and some palmist – to give you advance warning of what lies ahead!

Ancient palmistry filled these needs.

HOW ACCURATE IS IT?

The answer to this question has two parts. Remember that palmistry was the height of technology in its day, and served its purpose well enough to become deeply ingrained in the world's cultures. It was probably not much more – or less – inaccurate than much of our news and weather reports today. When you think about it, palmistry's information, provided on such a detailed and personal level, affected far fewer people than one inaccurate bit of news would today!

Then there was the invention of the printing press. The

development of printing is directly responsible for what we know of palmistry today. Until all the knowledge of palmistry could be preserved in the printed word, it could not be investigated as a science.

With mass-produced books, every facet of palmistry was available to all who could read. As a matter of fact, some of the very first books printed dealt with it. It became a scholarly subject at many universities. The good information became preserved, the inaccurate stuff was thrown out.

As a result, today we have a knowledge of palmistry that gives powerful and exciting insight into our natures, and our futures.

WHAT CAN YOU LEARN FROM PALMISTRY TODAY?

Many things! You can have the adventure of knowing yourself, your dreams and hopes, and the future that will spring from them.

You can learn about others in your life, getting a new slant on your loves, your family and friends. Even strangers become instantly familiar to you when you can see so much about them at a glance.

Palmistry enhances your insights in a simple and direct way. Whether you're choosing a job for yourself that best suits your skills or a mate to meet your needs, whether raising children to be the best they can be, helping friends, or entertaining yourself and others – all of this is easier and more effective with a grasp of the essentials of palmistry.

HOW DOES PALMISTRY WORK?

The key is in the focus on two issues – yourself and your future. Remember – one can't be understood without the other. Past events and conditions make you who you are, while the present holds the opportunities that create your future. In palmistry, the issue of time and the essence of self work together to build on past strengths, to correct weaknesses and steer a course for the future.

The 'past' in a hand includes:

- Heredity
- Character and personality
- Intelligence and temperament
- Talents
- Health
- Past events that shape present opportunities

The 'present' in a hand shows:

- Current personal needs
- How today's actions will affect the future
- How today's events will affect the future
- The best route to success

The 'future' in a hand reveals:

- Continued success or challenges in personal life
- Continued success or challenges in business life
- Lifestyle questions
- Questions about children or grandchildren

This book will show you how to get started. Before long, you too will be reading the secret language of the hands.

HOW TO BEGIN YOUR STUDY

At first glance, palmistry may seem a bit complicated. But if you keep your approach simple, you'll have no trouble picking it up. The material has a natural order to it, and following that order will help you keep the essentials in mind as you go along.

In palmistry, one detail, such as the size or shape of the hand, sets the foundation or background for the next group of information you'll receive. Everyone is interested in the lines, of course, but lines are analyzed last, after other features of the hands. This is because the meaning of the lines is modified by the type and size of hand they're in.

The best way to begin is to let your interest in hands take over as you explore the information I'm going to give you and compare it to your own hand and those of others. Each time you apply what you have learned to a hand, you will get the information more firmly in mind. Palmistry takes practice, but this doesn't stop anyone who is really interested. Remember, each hand has its own mysterious tale to tell.

When you see something in a hand that really attracts your curiosity and you find you can interpret it correctly, jot it down. Keep a record of what you discover. You can refer back to each detail you have mastered on your own.

You can also take this process a step further and set up a notebook for the hands you study. Choose five or six people you want to work with and devote a section of the notebook to each one. As you learn how to analyze their hands, step by step, keep notes.

It's a good idea to choose a variety of people to study, both people you know well and those who are less familiar to you. This way you can chart your progress in a more unbiased way. You want to prove to yourself that palmistry works. You'll really get a clear measure of your skill the day you decide to look at the hands of total strangers.

Some people make the transition from the early study of hands and practice on a close few, to reading for many strangers, to actually setting up a practice as a professional hand analyst. Long practice and dialogue with everyone whose hands you read makes this growth possible.

Hand prints: There's another record that will help you recall exactly what you find in a hand. Early in your studies, you may want to take hand prints. Prints let you see all the little details in the lines. This way you can study the palms at leisure, mark them and keep them for reference. What's more, lines do change. You'll welcome having the proof that they've done so if you keep a set of prints for yourself, update them about every six months and compare the differences over a period of time.

Get this equipment together before you begin:

- A glass baking dish or flat pan like a cookie sheet
- A tube of black water-soluble printer's ink
- A small hand roller, approximately 4½-6" in size
- A small towel
- Good typing paper

You can get the ink and hand roller at an art supply store. Be sure to ask for water-soluble ink.

Next, follow these simple steps:

1. Fold the towel to a square larger than your hand.

2. Center a piece of the typing paper over the towel.

3. Squeeze out a thin line of ink onto the pan or dish.

4. Use the roller to work the ink evenly over the pan's surface.

5. Put your hand gently down onto the inked surface of the pan.

6. Press gently on top of that hand with your other hand.

7. Carefully lift your hand up from the pan.

8. Check to see if the palm is completely inked. If not, take the ink-coated roller and apply it to the un-inked surface of your palm; and to your fingers, all the way to the tips, if they too have not been completely covered by the ink.

9. Gently lay your hand on the paper, then press firmly into the towel.

10. With your other hand, press the hand further into the towel.

11. Lift the palm slowly. The paper will stick to it.

12. With the paper still attached to your hand, rub the center of your palm carefully with the other hand to be sure the ink has transferred completely to the paper. (The center of the palm might not print if you skip this step.)

13. Slowly peel the paper from your hand.

14. Sign and date the prints.

15. Take an additional set of prints if any of the lines didn't come out to your satisfaction the first time.

THE BASICS OF PALMISTRY

As we've seen, lines aren't the only source of information in palmistry. The whole hand reveals our nature and our future. Features such as size, shape and length of the palm and fingers, along with color, skin texture and flexibility of the hand, further define the person. Everything that can be seen in a hand can be analyzed. And that's a lot!

What's more, the best palmists work with both sides of the hand. With this approach, you'll be able to learn a great deal more than if you stick to only part of the story – the palm.

The traditional starting point of analysis is to determine the size, shape, length and texture of the hand. Next, follow a similar procedure for the nails and fingers. Finally, evaluate the mounts and lines. Up-to-date palmistry also pays attention to the gestures used during normal conversation and the spaces between the hands and fingers when the hands are positioned on a flat surface, like a table top.

MAIN POINTS: These are the main points and the order in which to analyze them:

1. The size of the hands

2. The thickness of the palm

3. The shape of the palm

4. The length of the palm

5. Skin firmness, texture and color

6. Size, length, shape, color in the nails

7. Spaces between the hands and fingers

8. The length of the fingers

9. The shape of the fingertips

10. The mounts, their size, shape and marks

11. The lines

It's also important to observe gestures while you analyze hands. As you'll discover, they form a backdrop to the main work and add clues to a person's state of mind and feelings.

Now we'll take a look at the meanings for all these features.

THE HANDS

Size is the first thing you notice about a hand. Although most are about the same, you're bound to come across some hands that are distinctly large or small. These different sizes, in turn, spell out a distinct approach to life.

SMALL HANDS:
You are a lively soul, living at full tilt the adventure life has to offer. Your heightened senses and intuition lead the way in your decisions and desires. You enjoy taking risks, and as if by magic, you always land on your feet.

LARGE HANDS:
You look at life in great detail, analyzing every step you take. Your powers of concentration are an asset and your ability to complete any task you set yourself is admirable.

PALM THICKNESS: Now let's look at the thickness of the hands.

THICK HANDS:
People can count on finding you in the middle of the action because you are a doer. You have the drive and energy to achieve a high profile. You are a mover and a shaker.

THIN HANDS:
You are one of life's sensitive dreamers, alert to all that goes on around you. A tranquil environment helps recharge your batteries. You stop and smell the roses.

PALM SHAPE: The next feature in hand analysis is the shape of the palm itself. There are three separate shapes to be analyzed. Each palm has at least one of these shapes, and often a combination of them. The shape will tell a lot about your behavior and motivation.

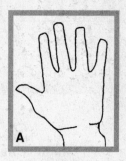

SQUARE

SQUARE PALMS: Square is the easiest shape to spot in a palm. The corners and edges are square, especially at the bottom of the palm. This shape means you're looking at the 'bottom line' in any discussion and are out for results. You want good value for your time and money. (**A**)

ROUND PALMS: A round shape is also easy to recognize because the outside edge of the hand has a curve to it. The corners of the palm will also be more round. People with palms this shape are fun-loving and sociable. People are drawn to your warmth and charm. In work or play, you are optimistic. You want to enjoy life. (**B**)

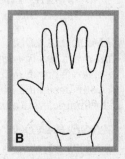

ROUND

SPATULATE PALMS: Spatulate is a wedge shape in which the bottom of the palm is wider than the top. Occasionally this is reversed, with the top half of the hand wider. In either form, this shape means you want the most out of life. You are restless, pioneering at heart, and not content until you have territory to call your own. Explorers who discovered new lands had this shape palm, and you share their desire for adventure. (**C**)

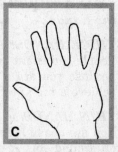

SPATULATE

16

PALM LENGTH: Meeting life's stresses and challenges is often a matter of adjustment. How flexible you are, how easily you adjust to change, is revealed by the length of your palm.

SHORT PALMS: A short palm is exactly as wide as it is long. A short palm is also a square palm because all four sides are equal. If your palm is short, you take life's bumps in stride, adjust quickly to change, and welcome challenge. You are a great help in any crisis because you know just what to do. You move fast. In day-to-day life, you also make quick decisions. You look forward to the future with a sense of anticipation. You like to take action! (**D**)

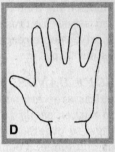

SHORT

LONG PALMS: A long palm is longer than it is wide. If your palm is long, you are most likely the family 'historian', remembering anniversaries, lovingly preserving family records and keepsakes. Your sense of reverence makes you treasure the past. You are often slow to adjust to new or challenging circumstances. 'Yesterday' appeals to you, and you like to take your time to make any decision that spells change in your life. (**E**)

LONG

17

FIRMNESS: The firmness of a hand helps us judge whether a person has enough strength to meet life's challenges.

FIRM HANDS: Those with hands that are firm to the touch have great strength. You are physically fit and emotionally able to respond to any stress. You resist pressure nicely. People respond to your leadership.

SOFT HANDS: When your palms are very soft, you give in rather easily to your feelings, to others, to any stress or challenge. People respond to your kind and sympathetic nature. Exercising both your body and your ability to say 'no' will increase your happiness.

TEXTURE: You determine skin texture by the back of the hand. You'll need to both feel and look at the skin to decide what type of texture it has.

There are three types of texture: fine, medium and coarse. Fine skin feels soft to the touch; medium, less so; and coarse skin has a noticeable resistance about it as you run your finger over the back of the hand. When you look carefully, you will notice some skin has visible pores, noticeable 'holes' all across it, and other skin appears to be like porcelain.

Fine skin looks like porcelain, with no pores visible; medium skin may have a few pores visible; coarse skin has very visible pores, and some hair on the hand as well — more, of course, on a man's hand than a woman's.

FINE SKIN: Naturally very sensitive, your powers tend to be mental and emotional. You are very interested in relating to others in harmony and comfort. You like a touch of luxury in your surroundings. When you are worried, you are likely to read a novel, eat your favorite food, or escape to the movies or a concert. You are not fond of physical activity or direct confrontation with others. You are subtle in your approach and make a good diplomat.

MEDIUM SKIN: Medium skin is a happy blend of the other two types. You have enough staying power for all you want to do, and you enjoy time spent in the company of others. You are open and flexible in your dealings with others, because you can meet challenges and stress head on.

COARSE SKIN: No one sign in the hand reveals more stamina and 'go power' than coarse skin. With this skin, you have an iron constitution and can hold up under great stress. You will need the outdoors and lots of physical activity to work off excess energy. When you have worries, you tend to be physically active to help you cope. You resist emotional and verbal pressure from others. You are independent and make up your own mind on matters.

COLOR: Color in the palm is important, too. Pink is the preferred color for a palm, showing happiness and health. Theoretically, the pink color should cover the palm evenly. But in reality we all have patches of deeper or lighter tones spread throughout the palm.

PINK PALMS: If your palms are mainly pink, then you are happy and cheerful and feel good about yourself and your life.

PALE PALMS: If your palms are pale, your energy level is a little low. You need time by yourself to recharge after a demanding day.

SPECKLED PALMS: Some palms have what appear to be little white speckles running along their surface. These spots show strong emotions that are not being expressed. Some time alone to think, dream and release your feelings will clear up these spots.

THE NAILS

Nail Size: After a look at skin texture, take a look at the nails. Their size, length and shape tell a lot about your energy and temperament, as well as what type of activity and job will suit you best.

LARGE NAILS:

You have great physical energy and endurance, as well as a steady personality. Like people with coarse skin, you need physical outlets for your energy. You'd enjoy a hobby or craft that demands manual dexterity, such as engraving, wood working or carpentry. You can easily work a 10-hour day – and go out on the town at night. (**A**)

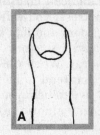

SMALL NAILS:

You are famous for your child-like personality, your urge for fun and variety. You are spontaneous and well liked, and you would do well in any job with an emphasis on contact with people. Your energy rises and falls, which means you won't always be able to work all day and party all night. You know this and will make your choices according to your energy level. (**B**)

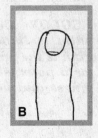

NAIL LENGTH: Nail length is measured from the base of the nail, up the sides, and up to the tip of the finger. The ends that extend past the finger itself don't count as length. As with the guidelines for palm length, long nails are longer than they are wide, and short nails are as wide as they are long.

LONG NAILS: Because you love to dream, you see and create possibilities in ways that others don't. Your expanded view of reality makes you a natural at counseling and inspiring others. You follow your own instincts as you establish the rhythm of your life and achievements. You most likely have artistic ability. Check it out. (**C**)

SHORT NAILS: You are a real dynamo, buzzing around, involved in several projects at once, wanting all of them finished yesterday. You don't like to gamble on theories and promises; you want results now! In your practical, constructive approach to life, you can accomplish more than the average person. You do well in business. It's important for you to take time to relax for yourself and family on a regular basis. (**D**)

NAIL SHAPE: The shape of your nails is measured the same way the length is. Look at the bottom and the sides of each nail. The bottom of the nail gives you the best clue to shape. There are three possible shapes: round, square and flared. A round nail looks oval; a square nail has perfectly straight edges at the sides, and a flared (spatulate) nail has a characteristic 'V' shape.

When you understand nail shape, you are ahead of the game in your interaction with others because you have a handle on how a person will act and why. This insight gives you a competitive edge in business and clues to the needs of your friends and lovers.

ROUND NAILS: Friendly, intuitive and adaptable, you can be counted on to give everyone a fair chance. You love to study people, and your social life is important to you. You keep in touch with the latest trends and fashions. People and entertainment are important to you. A new venture appeals to you if it promises to be fun. (**E**)

SQUARE NAILS: You can be a perfectionist, especially in your work and matters you think are most important – such as buying a house or raising children. You expect a lot of yourself, and you have a lot to give in return. Your technical skills hasten your advancement to the top of your field. You tend to be organized and appreciate schedules. A new venture will appeal to you if it seems useful. (**F**)

SPATULATE NAILS: If you have anything to say about it, you never know a dull moment. Restless, curious and enthusiastic, you will try most anything once. Companies, your own or those of others, benefit from your pioneering skills. At home, you avoid being tied down to routine. Adventure, travel – any new horizon fires your imagination and determination to succeed. You have an original view of the world, and faced with a new venture, your first question is: "Has this been done before?" If not, you'd like to be the first. (**G**)

> **NOTE:** Nail shape also gives a clue to health. But these shapes are out of the ordinary, so we won't deal with them in this limited space.

NAIL COLOR: *Color in both the palms and the nails gives a clue to health and happiness.*

If you have a light pink tone under your nails, your health and vitality are excellent. A pale or white color is a signal that you are going on nervous energy, and might do well to look into a tonic to boost your iron level and energy. A purple color near the moon of the nail indicates the possibility of fatigue. If you notice this color in your nails, take a weekend off to restore your energy.

GESTURES & POSTURES

As you talk with another person, information comes to you on two levels, both verbally (through speech) and non-verbally (through body movement). When you receive non-verbal input from someone's hands, the information goes directly into your brain, usually without your even realizing it. This type of non-verbal communication is known as body language.

Palmistry's approach to non-verbal communication can be understood as the study of body language in miniature. The difference is that body language analyzes the hands' motions, or gestures, while palmistry interprets them while they're still, that is, their postures. In either case, the hands' natural positioning tells you where a person is coming from.

Hand gestures and postures add a special dimension to the study of palmistry. For this type of analysis, you'll need to watch for clues even before you begin a formal reading. To form a basis for understanding many of the hands' gestures, you may want to check any of the books on body language available today. These meanings will deepen your understanding of your client before you begin to analyze the hands' postures.

Is your client comfortable, confident and assured? Or does he or she have self-doubts or doubts about the future? You can see why it would be helpful to have a clue to a person's attitude before you begin your analysis of his or her hands.

How do hand postures work? Begin by asking your client to put his hands palms down on a table top. You're going to analyze the spaces between the hands, then those between the fingers.

***HANDS ON THE TABLE:** The first thing to consider is whether or not the hands lie flat on the table.*

HANDS FLAT: If they remain flat, with the fingers stretched out all the way, then the person feels very secure – and the request to do something unusual hasn't thrown him at all. He no doubt expected you to look at his palms.

He feels good. Things are looking up. If a challenge comes his way, he knows he can handle it because he's strong and confident. **(A)**

HANDS RAISED: If the hands form an arch, with the fingers and palms cupped on the table, then the person has a lot on his mind. Your unexpected request makes him reveal the uncertainty he feels about both it and the issues on his mind. He feels he can't be sure of anything right now.

His life is changing, and he wants to make the most of his opportunities. He'll do so by remaining poised and flexible and by meeting uncertainty head on. **(B)**

The previous interpretations apply when you look at both hands together. The next step is to analyze the hands separately as they stay in their original position.

NOTE: If your subject is right-handed, the right hand represents three months ahead in time, and the left hand represents the past three months. If he's left-handed, just reverse the interpretations that follow:

RIGHT HAND FLAT... LEFT HAND ARCHED: Three months ago, life had its uncertain moments for you. Everything you wondered about then has apparently settled down now, and you are free to proceed without the concerns you had then.

RIGHT HAND ARCHED... LEFT HAND FLAT: Three months ago, you were sailing through life. But now, a few questions have come up. You'll spend the next three months getting answers to those questions – or 'setting your ducks in a row', so to speak.

SPACES BETWEEN THE HANDS: The clues we have just seen tell how secure you feel about your present situ-ation. The next clue reveals what you'll do about that situation. The space between the hands as they're positioned on the table indicates how ready you are to take action.

HANDS HELD WIDE APART: You are ready to act now and will tolerate no delays. You're eager and confident.

HANDS PLACED CLOSE TOGETHER: You feel cautious. You want to buy a little time before you act. You'll think twice about your options.

Remember, how flat the hands lie on the table tells how secure you feel; how wide apart the hands are held reveals your readiness to take action. One last question remains. What will fate think of your ideas and desires?

ALIGNMENT: Your two hands as they're positioned on the table will either be in exact alignment with one another or one hand will be positioned a bit higher than the other.

25

This hand appears to 'take the lead' by being in front of the other, poking out a little, and breaking the alignment of all the fingers.

This posture represents your unconscious knowledge of the way events will turn out over the next three months. We do know the future – we're simply not consciously aware of it. In this case, the hands tell us what we need to know.

RIGHT HAND PLACED AHEAD OF THE LEFT:

This is a sign of progress. The coming three months will go very well. Everything you plan will happen easily and without interruption. Your plans come to success. This is a sure 'go' signal.

LEFT HAND PLACED AHEAD OF THE RIGHT:

This signals delay. For the next three months, you may expect delays. This is not the time to get everything you desire accomplished. Expect to rearrange plans to make up for any obstacles or minor annoyances you may encounter.

BOTH HANDS PLACED EVENLY:

You've got a green light. You are ready for anything and will successfully

complete all tasks.

FINGER SPACES: Perhaps the most fun of all are the quick clues you get from the spaces between the fingers. You can see these at the same time you are checking out the hands' posture on the table, as we have just done.

As the hands rest on the table, the fingers will either be held close together or spread wide apart.

FINGER SPACES WIDE:

This is a confident time. You love life and revel in its pressures. You have confidence in yourself and know you can handle any challenge. Each day is a new adventure!

FINGER SPACES NARROW:

This is a sign of caution. You take care of yourself and deal with life very seriously. A hard worker, you would rather walk a mile than make a mistake. Your careful, conscientious approach to life will reward you.

PARTICULAR FINGER SPACES:

In addition, each of the spaces between your fingers has a meaning that gives more definition to your personality. The space between the index and middle fingers shows whether you're an independent thinker. Between the middle and ring fingers, the space reveals how you spend your money. And the last space, the one between the ring and little fingers, indicates how independent your actions are.

WIDE SPACE BETWEEN INDEX AND MIDDLE: You're a free thinker. You think quickly, make up your own mind, and do not like interference with your plans. If people ask you for your opinion, you will give it.

NARROW SPACE BETWEEN INDEX AND MIDDLE: A deliberate person, you like to check your facts before you speak. And you don't often reveal all you are thinking. When you consider a new venture, you move slowly.

WIDE SPACE BETWEEN MIDDLE AND RING: This is the sign of a lavish spender. Money speaks, and you like its language. You spend generously because you're confident of your earning power.

NARROW SPACE BETWEEN MIDDLE AND RING: You hang onto money because you feel your finances are tight. You tend to put off spending for anything that's not essential.

WIDE SPACE BETWEEN RING AND LITTLE: An action sign! You can act first, think later. You are impulsive, and won't be held back. You are courageous, taking the first step where others hang back.

NARROW SPACE BETWEEN RING AND LITTLE: You're disciplined. You know those times in your life when you just have to buckle down. You're willing to make sacrifices right now, giving up something in the immediate future in order to gain more later.

NOTE: The spaces between the fingers may not be the same on both hands. Say the space between the index and middle fingers on the right hand isn't the same as that on the left hand. In that case, you can use the same time frame you used for the hands' positions. The message of the fingers on the right hand will be true for the next three months. The meanings from the left hand were true for the last three months. Once again, left-handed subjects need to switch meanings.

THE FINGERS

We've seen how palmistry uses a form of body language to understand the motionless posture of the hands. Next we're going to concentrate on a 'still life' version of the fingers, analyzing their length and shape.

FINGER LENGTH:

Have you ever been told your fingers are 'long'? Do you know someone who says: "Oh, my fingers look so stubby"? Either of these statements might be true. The only way to tell is to measure them. In palmistry, the fingers' length is determined by how it compares to the length of the palms. Typically, the palms are longer than the fingers.

HOW TO MEASURE FINGER LENGTH:

It's not necessary to measure all the fingers. Use the middle one as a guide. With a ruler, measure the length of that finger. Then measure the length of your palm for comparison.

AVERAGE FINGERS:

The average finger length takes up three-quarters of the palm. Fingers longer than that mark are considered 'long', while those that don't reach the three-quarters mark are considered 'short'. Fingers that are as long as the palm itself are classified 'very long'.

SHORT FINGERS:

Your short fingers mean you're a live wire! Enthusiastic, impatient and eager for experience, you have the ability to 'wing it', to go straight to the heart of matters. Your ability to stick to essentials and to act quickly complements your strong intuitive powers. In business, you have great potential as a manager.

LONG FINGERS:

If your fingers are long, you have the temperament of a specialist. You like to analyze all sides of a situation before you act. You are patient, thorough and loyal. You take great pride in doing your work well. You truly value your friendships. Though you may not make friends easily, once a person is your friend, he is your friend for life.

THE THUMB'S LENGTH:

In palmistry, the thumb is measured separately from the other fingers. To measure your thumb, hold it against the side of your hand, close to the index finger. The tip of the average-length thumb comes to a point halfway up the bottom section of the index finger. If the thumb falls short of that mark, it is 'short'. Longer than the halfway mark means the thumb is 'long'.

LONG THUMBS:

A long thumb indicates strong willpower. Dependable and achievement-oriented, you do what you promise you will. Once you give your word, you carry through.

SHORT THUMBS:

A short thumb means you enjoy life and the people around you. You often let others make decisions. You don't respond to pressure in a combative way, preferring to be diplomatic and to find a way to keep the peace.

***FINGERTIP SHAPE:** Fingertip shape reveals personality. Traditionally, the shape has been used to denote your abilities and temperament. Today we can also say that this shape reflects your inner drive and sense of purpose.*

The three main shapes for fingernails – flared (spatulate), square and round – also apply to the fingertips. In addition, fingertips can be pointed.

Here is a brief guide to fingertip shapes and their general meanings. Later, we will apply these meanings to each individual fingertip.

FLARED FINGERTIPS: Flared tips signal a drive toward achievement and accomplishment. With these tips, you will be in a hurry, feeling the pressure of all that you want to create. You won't be satisfied until you have conquered the world – or at least your corner of it. Any hint of adventure or challenge spurs you on. (**A**)

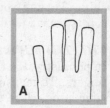

SQUARE FINGERTIPS: With square fingertips, you will want to focus on results and the bottom line. You like to play by the rules. Being conservative, you appreciate tradition and a sense of security. Your great desire is to be productive and to have something to show for your time. (**B**)

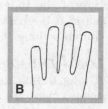

ROUND FINGERTIPS: You are adaptable. You're also flexible enough to try several routes to success in life because you love variety. All of your best experiences and memories will include people – because people are very important to you. (**C**)

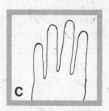

POINTED FINGERTIPS: You have the soul of a beautiful dreamer. You respond to the unusual and have a rhythm to your life that differs from the ordinary. Poets, artists and performers have fingertips like yours. (**D**)

Each finger has a name of its own. To better portray what the fingers mean, the ancients gave them the names out of mythology. These names were a kind of code word for a certain sort of energy.

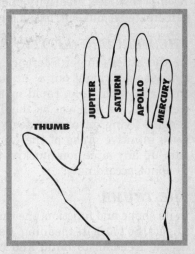

● Index finger: *Jupiter*; Middle finger: *Saturn*; Ring finger: *Apollo*; Little finger: *Mercury*. The thumb has no special name and is analyzed differently from the other fingers.

Today we have the option of using the old names or referring to the fingers by the names we know. For now, let's use both names as we look at the significance of each finger.

THE JUPITER (INDEX) FINGER:

Jupiter is the strongest finger. It's so easy to use that little children first express themselves and their desires instinctively, raising this finger to point toward an object. With adults, the 'pointer' finger reveals the way a person succeeds in the world. What kind of life and career does a person want? This finger also expresses authority and leadership.

THE SATURN (MIDDLE) FINGER:

Usually the longest finger on a hand, the middle finger stands rather like a sentinel in a tower, surveying the landscape that lies below. Traditionally, this finger is associated with caution, balance and conscience. Saturn shows a person's sense of responsibility and mind set.

31

THE APOLLO (RING) FINGER:

Apollo has neither the freedom of movement that Jupiter does, nor the length of Saturn. Standing in a world of its own between the tallest finger and the littlest finger, Apollo represents romance, creativity and the environment each person can create for himself, based on his or her ability to be happy.

THE MERCURY (LITTLE) FINGER:

As the littlest finger, Mercury can move subtly from side to side, shoot straight out at an angle and fold or curve toward the palm with agile, rapid motion. The god Mercury, in ancient lore, was known as the Trickster. He was also a messenger, flying on winged feet. This finger expresses a person's intuitive grasp of the world around him, the ability to sum up any situation quickly, to diagnose any problem, and to adapt accordingly.

THE THUMB:

In its shape and function, the thumb is different from the other fingers. So too is its meaning. Because the human thumb gives us the freedom to build and choose in a way that sets us apart from other species, it has come to represent our will.

INDIVIDUAL FINGER LENGTH: Although we have examined the overall length of the fingers, there is one more detail to cover before we can put together the big picture of the fingers' meanings. Each individual finger should be in proportion to the others, as well. The index and ring fingers should each be half a tip shorter than the middle finger, and the little finger should reach exactly to the line that divides the top section of the ring finger from the rest. (**A**)

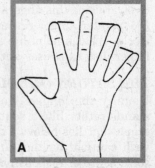

The length and shape of each finger adds to their essential meanings. Check each of your fingers for length and shape of the tip then compare them with the descriptions that follow:

JUPITER FINGER LENGTH AND SHAPE:

A long Jupiter finger means that you are confident. Even at an early age, you're a natural authority figure with plenty of leadership ability. You assume responsibility and will easily rise to the top of your field. You may be singled out for honors and attention. You make your way easily in the world.

● With a short Jupiter finger, you are comfortable acting behind the scenes, where you help others who are more ambitious or comfortable with the limelight. Because you are very good at planning strategy, you are a skilled and desirable adviser. You often feel shy, but your interest in people and issues is genuine, and you welcome a chance to be of service. You make a difference in the lives of others – quietly.

● Tip shape shows how you approach your career or any effort at success. Square tips are detail-oriented, conscientious, and work well with established guidelines; round tips mean you are impressionable and adapt well to change; flared tips concentrate on how much impact they can make with any new project; pointed tips are a sign of a receptive nature and a desire to make people feel at ease in their work.

SATURN FINGER LENGTH AND SHAPE:

With a long Saturn finger, your natural caution and desire for security make you debate the 'ins-and-outs' of any new venture before you will commit. You like answers and reasonable explanations for any questions you may have. With your philosophical turn of mind, you can successfully guide a new business to a solid performance.

● A short Saturn finger reveals that you are carefree and have a yen for experience that makes you leery of any venture that ties you down. You will experience a lot of life before you settle into a routine that gives you security and stability. This sign often means you'll have two different

33

careers, one early in life and another later, as your experience influences the goals you will choose.

● Here, tip shape shows how you will go about doing any task, from the most ordinary to the most creative. A square tip needs good order to create and contribute to life and will stick to details, using a methodical, organized approach. Round tips are more relaxed about their tasks, knowing somehow they will all get done. A flared tip has a deep need to be original and innovative. A pointed tip will set its own terms for performance. This last shape on Saturn is rare.

APOLLO FINGER LENGTH AND SHAPE:

Those who have long Apollo fingers show a natural enthusiasm and capacity for joy, especially in any artistic or creative field that gives you a special charm. You seem to have the secret of life at your fingertips. People love to be around you because you are warm and radiant, and attract luck and love.

● With short Apollo fingers, you need a little prodding to believe in yourself and to see yourself as others do. The support of family and friends leads you out of your shell to claim a bit of the world for yourself. Once you find an interest that you love, you will devote all your time and energy to it.

● Square tips on Apollo cut down on the desire to take risks; round tips increase the desire for social life and people contact. Flared tips signal an inventive person who can gain recognition as a performer. Successful sculptors also have these tips. Pointed Apollo tips indicate a flighty type of person, but one whose heart is full of love and enthusiasm.

MERCURY FINGER LENGTH AND SHAPE:

If you have a long Mercury finger, you are the most persuasive of people. You know just how to get to the heart of the matter, to capture the attention of anyone you wish to convince. You would do well in sales, politics, or in any career where you earn your living through words and ideas. In the best of the type, you have polish, refinement and suave ways that will win you prizes and a comfortable life.

● If your Mercury finger is short, you pride yourself on your 'down-home' manners. You believe that folks are just folks. You are blunt, humorous and quick to anger. Although you 'tell it like it is', you are earnest and often childlike. You win people over with your aura of openness and vulnerability.

● With square tips, you perform well in any technical field. Round tips add a touch of intuition to your communication skills. Flared tips reveal your restless nature, and a pointed tip has qualities similar to the long finger. Your pleasing ways, quick mind and ability to make others feel good assure success.

THUMB LENGTH AND SHAPE:

Your long thumb is your calling card to success. You are highly motivated and won't take no for an answer. You should have your own business, or a lot of freedom in your work. You pace yourself well and make it a point to reach the goal you set for yourself.

● With a short thumb, you have a less determined personality. You have to make a conscious effort to stick to the goals you set for yourself. You work well with deadlines and with the support of others to boost your self-confidence. The love and approval of others works wonders, helping you go far in life.

● The square shape is most often found on thumbs, increasing determination and courage in the face of trouble. Round tips show a mild nature. This is a tolerant, understanding person. Flared tips are famous for their impatience. Pointed tips are rare, but show a person likely to look to life's experience to teach him, rather than feeling he is master of his own fate.

THE MOUNTS

Mounts are the little raised areas on the surface of the palm. If you look carefully at your palm, you'll see how the entire surface is not flat, but curved in spots where the contours, or mounts, stand out. These contours define the personality and potential of a person just as a desert or mountain defines a physical place and the activities appropriate to it.

The mounts and lines work together in a good hand analysis. Lines pass through or around the mounts, and the mounts themselves have small lines on them.

There are seven mounts representing seven different types of personalities. Like the fingers, each mount has a name symbolic of the energy it represents. You'll find the names and location of the mounts in the palm to the left, and then the type of approach to life each mount depicts.

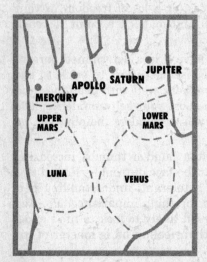

Jupiter/Leader
Saturn/Thinker
Apollo/Creator
Mercury/Genius
Venus/Lover
Mars/Fighter
Luna/Dreamer

The best developed mount in our hands reveals our 'type' and the abilities associated with that type. To determine which mount is the best, pick the one that stands up high and is firm to the touch. Height and firmness are the qualities that show a well-developed mount.

Occasionally, a hand has more than one well-developed mount. In that case, simply note the mounts and combine their qualities. After all, a person can be both a 'dreamer' and a 'creator', or a 'leader' and a 'thinker'. If two mounts stand equally high in the hand, be sure they are also equally firm to the touch before you decide that both are equally developed.

A high mount means that you have those qualities in you, while a firm one shows you are using those qualities. If a mount is flat or soft, its qualities and potential are either not present or they're not being used. Using the potential that is in you makes the mounts grow firm.

Here's a profile of the traits and abilities associated with each mount:

THE JUPITER MOUNT:

Jupiter has ambition, drive, a strong ego, and a desire for achievement. He's found in high profile positions, as a leader or teacher or executive. He is generous, volunteering time and money to many causes. He has an interest in religion or spiritual life. He sets high standards for himself and others. Honor and integrity matter deeply to him.

● A few of the careers in which he'll excel are teaching, politics, public speaking, administration, publishing, diplomacy and the food service industry.

THE SATURN MOUNT:

Saturn has a love of solitude. He needs time to think and ponder over life's mysteries. He is a good investigator or philosopher who is known for his wise and cautious ways. He is very conservative and likes to live close to the land, or wherever there is peace, quiet, order and harmony in everyday life. He can be reclusive and doesn't need any frills.

● Saturn makes a good analyst, researcher, mathematician or scientist. Other good career choices are geology, geophysics, metallurgy, agriculture and ecology.

THE APOLLO MOUNT:

Apollo is a performer, a star, in any territory. Warm, full of joy and spontaneity, he attracts notice. He likes the spotlight, and is often the center of an admiring circle of friends. He is versatile and artistic, in love with the beauty and drama of life. Love, laughter, creativity and a taste for the extraordinary are his trademarks.

● His best career choices are artist, actor or performer; art gallery or arts and crafts shop owner or museum director. He'll also excel in film or video, music or the entertainment industry, sales, advertising and public relations. He is a good makeup artist, image consultant, designer or interior decorator.

THE MERCURY MOUNT:

Mercury's chief traits are quickness of mind, shrewdness and penetrating insight. Not much escapes his notice. Good in business, he manages money and plans marketing strategy well. He is quite the deal maker. He is sometimes intellectual and often a very eloquent speaker. Full of wit and humor, he knows just how to motivate others.

● Mercury excels as an entrepreneur and pioneer. He is found in all professional fields, including business, banking and finance. Medicine appeals to him, as well as psychiatry. He also does well as a psychologist, therapist or social worker, writer, editor, or gossip columnist. He is often also found in aviation.

THE VENUS MOUNT:

Venus qualities include a love of life, an abundance of energy, a strong feeling for home and family, and a love of humanity. Venus is tender, sympathetic and impulsive, as well as affectionate and a peacemaker. Venus is often sexy and exuberant, and loves music, dance and beauty. Comfort and luxury appeal to him.

● Venus does well in the beauty and fashion industries, as well as in the arts. Music, dance and the theater are all good choices, as well as any field connected with the creation and maintenance of the home. Careers as a teacher of small children, a marriage counselor, or family therapist satisfy Venus. Planning social events and working as a recreation director are further avenues to success.

THE LUNA MOUNT:

Luna is by nature mysterious, a bit withdrawn and, at times, secretive. Great inner longings, a poetic view of life and a love for travel preoccupy him. He is fascinated by romance, fiction, distant horizons, nature and scenery, and the rhythms and cycles of creation. He is often psychic and intuitive.

● Luna's career potential is shaped by an ability for language and symbols. Poetry, drama, music, languages, and writing offer chances for fulfillment. Most composers have a strong Luna mount. In addition, meditation, yoga, and hypnotherapy appeal to Luna. A love of travel can make him a success in both an import/export business and the transportation industry.

THE MARS MOUNT:

You may have noticed that Mars appears in two places in the hand, once near the thumb, and again at the outside edge of the hand. The first Mars is 'lower Mars' and the second is known as 'upper Mars'. Both mounts express courage and determination. But the energy represented by 'lower Mars' is aggressive, while the energy of 'upper Mars' is passive.

LOWER MARS:

This Mars mount is ambitious and highly motivated. He loves a good fight or challenge. He likes nothing better than the chance to prove himself. 'Initiative' is the key word here.

● Lower Mars is good at athletics, and especially at something rugged like trekking, mountain climbing or leading expeditions in the great outdoors. Handy in an emergency and blessed with quick reflexes, this type makes an excellent fireman, paramedic or surgeon, and is often found in the military. A career in business also focuses Mars' dynamic energy.

UPPER MARS:

Here we see the soul of patience, a person who is calm, persevering, steady, dependable and who resists pressure from any quarter. A nurturing type, upper Mars is helpful to others and follows through in any project. The chief quality is courage.

● Upper Mars is good in any communication field, personnel management or administration. This type does well in manufacturing and production, and is often found in heavy equipment sales and other businesses. Any job that requires a steady hand, such as arts, crafts, engraving, assembling small parts, or steady nerves, such as air traffic control, is a natural for this Mars.

As I've said, there is a difference in meaning between a good mount – one that is high and firm – and an undeveloped mount, which is flat or soft.

HIGH, FIRM JUPITER MOUNT:

You stand out in a crowd. People count on you to get the job done – professionally, socially and at home. You are self-assured.

SOFT, FLAT JUPITER MOUNT:

You have a gentle, timid approach to life and hesitate to take over anyone's 'territory'. You are sympathetic, a good listener, and help others on a personal, one-to-one basis.

HIGH, FIRM SATURN MOUNT:

You have great powers of concentration. You bring forth your best efforts to meet challenges – if you decide the cause is worthwhile, that is. You work with precision.

SOFT, FLAT SATURN MOUNT:

You are very determined, but you don't always look before you leap. You learn by experience. You are fearless and live by your own rules.

HIGH, FIRM APOLLO MOUNT:

You have a fabulous sense of art, form and color. Use your decorating skills to make your environment warm and cheerful.

SOFT, FLAT APOLLO MOUNT:

You enjoy watching creativity in the making – in films, theater and dance. You know hard work pays off, but it helps to visualize the rewards in advance to spur you on to greater heights.

HIGH, FIRM MERCURY MOUNT:

You are a dynamo! People respond to your words and you excel as a teacher or a salesperson. Along with selling ideas or products, you sell yourself, too, because you connect well with others through your intuition.

SOFT, FLAT MERCURY MOUNT:

When communicating with others, you must make yourself clear and establish basic ground rules. This way your transactions won't be confusing, nor your words misunderstood. You are also extremely intuitive, so try to use it to your best advantage!

HIGH, FIRM VENUS MOUNT:

With your energy, you can work all day and dance all night. Your family means a lot to you, and somehow you have the ability to 'do it all'.

SOFT, FLAT VENUS MOUNT:

You observe life closely. You may appear quiet, but others have a lot to learn from you, for you have taken the time to know yourself.

HIGH, FIRM LUNA MOUNT:

You love a mystery, whether you find it in a book, in a person, in nature – or in yourself! With your imagination, life is always an adventure.

SOFT, FLAT LUNA MOUNT:

You concentrate on essentials, bread on the table, a roof over your head. You develop your inner resources as you go along, gradually achieving security and serenity.

HIGH, FIRM LOWER MARS MOUNT:

Watch out, world! Your energy comes from super-octane fuel, designed to power the engine of your desires. You win out over obstacles with the strength of your will.

SOFT, FLAT LOWER MARS MOUNT:

This is the sign of persistence! You are capable of getting ahead when you follow your goals, one step at a time. Any positive feedback you get only increases your determination.

HIGH, FIRM UPPER MARS MOUNT:

You are confident and brave. You meet any surprise or adversity with a presence of mind that automatically sweeps your way clear.

SOFT, FLAT UPPER MARS MOUNT:

Challenge is good for you. Each time you win a battle, you are surprised and delighted. Sometimes you're tense, but your alertness has won the day for you, most likely more than once!

MARKS ON THE MOUNTS:

Small lines and marks on the mounts add an interesting sidelight to their essential meanings. Here are the types of lines and marks that appear on mounts along with their significance:

VERTICAL LINES increase the positive meaning of the mount.

HORIZONTAL LINES show an obstacle to fulfilling the talents of the mount.

SLANTED OR DIAGONAL LINES are 'influence' lines, bringing luck and people into your projects.

SINGLE BAR LINES mean obstacles or challenges in the area the mount represents.

GRILLES show confusion about your goals in the area represented by the mount.

CROSSES indicate a particular challenge, or at times, a special ability related to the mount.

SQUARES protect your talents.

TRIANGLES mean creativity in using the talent of the mount.

CIRCLES AND STARS are unusual, revealing unexpected circumstances, or recognition for your efforts.

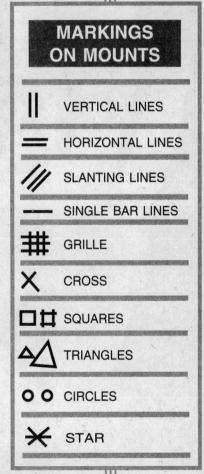

MARKINGS ON MOUNTS

‖	VERTICAL LINES
═	HORIZONTAL LINES
⫽	SLANTING LINES
—	SINGLE BAR LINES
▦	GRILLE
✕	CROSS
▢ ⊟	SQUARES
◹ △	TRIANGLES
○ ○	CIRCLES
✳	STAR

THE LIFE LINE

Because of their mysterious reputation for revealing the future, the lines are particularly fascinating to people interested in palmistry. Everybody wants to find out: "How long will I live?" or "Will I marry?"

Can you answer those questions from the lines? Just what do the lines reveal? How do they work?

The lines reveal a great deal, but they stop short of answering in exact detail a question about the length of life, at least in today's version of palmistry. They reveal marriage, for example, but the up-to-date view doesn't recognize the old approach of 'one marriage line, one marriage', or 'two marriage lines, two marriages'. The sections on the life line and relationship lines will explain this in more detail.

"Can the lines change?" is another common question. They can, and they do. But not all of them change to the same degree. The three major lines change least of all, and the rest of them, especially the smallest ones, alter their appearance over a period of time.

To someone just getting acquainted with palmistry, keeping track of the lines and interpreting them seems like a big job. But there is a way to keep it simple. Understand that any line, from the life line to the smallest line, consists of a designated starting point, a designated end and the route between the two points. Along the way, between the beginning and the end, a line will vary in its appearance. It is these variations, along with the two fixed points, that reveal a line's meaning.

The major lines are the life, heart and head lines. They are accompanied by the fate, Apollo and Mercury lines, along with

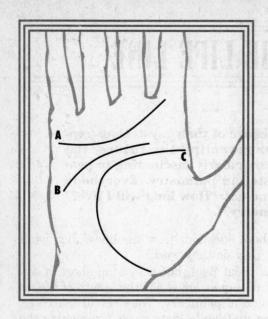

THE MAJOR LINES

A. Heart line
B. Head line
C. Life line

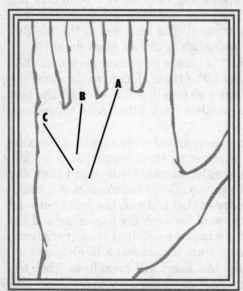

THE MINOR LINES

A. Fate line
B. Apollo line
C. Mercury line

special little lines and marks on the palm. For the purposes of this small book, we will concentrate on the first six lines.

To get you acquainted with each line, we'll learn the basic meanings and look at features such as length, curve, beginning and ending points. You'll soon see how these patterns add to the essential meaning of the lines.

THE LIFE LINE: The life line has to be treated with caution, for rarely does it reveal the length of life. That idea has come down through the ages, and while it may once have been possible to predict the length of life from a single line in the palm, today that's considered a far-fetched idea.

Before you get too disappointed, let's try to put this into perspective. After all, not even your doctor, your minister or Albert Einstein could answer such a question. Why would a palmist know how to do it? If there were a secret source for this knowledge in our information-hungry age, wouldn't another branch of science also have discovered it?

All fields of inquiry have been shaped by the amount of research and technology available today, and the message of the life line is no exception. The boundaries of the world we live in affect the way we apply what we know. Advances in medical science as well as our changing lifestyles make the old rules for gauging the length of life from the hand a whole new ball game.

There is one true message about the length of life in the life line, however. It holds a record of how long our ancestors lived. A long line means our ancestors had a long life span, and that we have inherited the probability of a long life. A short life line may once have meant we stood to have a shorter life, based on our genetic inheritance.

But medical science hasn't stood still over the last decades. Let's say your grandfather died of tuberculosis, or even the flu. You are very much less likely to do so today. His record, then, doesn't 'compute' as your potential life span. The same would be true if your ancestors all lived long lives in a quiet, remote town, and never exposed themselves to the risks we have in our lifestyle today. Our highways, crowded and dangerous, are a menace our forefathers never knew. Their long lives and your long life line are not a guarantee that an accident of any type will not occur.

Your life line describes your physical heredity, including physical strength and prospects for health. With its marks and variations as it crosses the palm, the line will reveal much of your early childhood, relationship with your parents, education, first experience at work, and your future chances for success. Travel and changes of residence can also be predicted.

The life line is also used to tell time. Using the diagram that appears later in this section, you will be able to tell when past conditions occurred and to pinpoint future events.

LOCATING THE LIFE LINE: The line that circles the thumb is the life line. It begins at the outside edge of the hand, under the index finger, and travels to the bottom of the palm.

BEGINNING PATTERNS: The life line typically begins under the Jupiter mount, at the outside edge of the hand. Occasionally, this line begins right on the Jupiter mount.

ENDING PATTERNS: The typical life line ends at the bottom of the palm, but others stop short of that, anywhere from halfway down the palm to just short of the average ending.

PATH ALONG THE PALM: The typical life line has a curve as it travels down the palm. That curve will either be narrow or wide. Occasionally, the line appears to flatten out. Sometimes, the line travels in a diagonal path, breaking out of the circular pattern that is the norm.

INTERPRETING THE PATTERNS

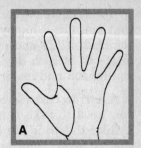

● A life line beginning at the outside edge of the hand shows normal ambition. (**A**)

● A life line beginning right on the Jupiter mount shows extreme ambition. If your life line begins there, you will go to the top of your field. (**B**)

● If your life line goes all the way to the bottom of your hand, you are blessed with energy and health, and can go forward full throttle in life. (**C**)

● If your life line stops shortly before the bottom of the palm, a little care and precaution will see you through even the most demanding of days. (**D**)

● A life line that stops halfway down the palm tells you to watch your diet, exercise, rest, and keep a positive attitude. You have a tendency to run yourself ragged. Make a point to take time to relax. You have a strong sense of adventure and like to take risks whenever they present themselves. (**E**)

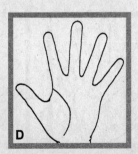

49

● A wide curve to your life line reveals that you are a happy, outgoing person, full of life and eager to get the most out of each day. People look to you for fun and inspiration. (**F**)

● A narrow curve in a life line means you need to take time for yourself. Unlike the wide curve that reveals the extrovert, you keep to yourself and like your own space. (**G**)

● If your life line is more flat than curved, you tend to be shy. But once you find your niche and work at something interesting, you succeed. (**H**)

● A life line that juts out on a diagonal track is a great line for adventure and travel. You will move often in your lifetime and will live a lifestyle very different from your parents. (**I**)

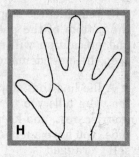

Two additional variations are sometimes present in life lines. The line can be double or it can shift course.

● A double life line means you can recuperate from almost any illness. The line is a safety net and is sometimes called the 'antibody line'. (**J**)

● If the life line stops halfway down to the palm, breaks away and resumes a new course down to the bottom of the palm, this is

the surest sign of a move – either a change of residence locally or a move as far away as possible. (**K**)

TIME ON THE LIFE LINE: With a little practice, you will soon be able to tell time on the life line. Take a look at the diagram with the different years and their place on the line.

The first step is to trace an imaginary line down the middle of your middle finger from the top to the point where the line intersects the life line. This is age 35 on your hand. (**L**)

● Because so much is packed into our early years, including our childhood, education, first jobs, career, marriage choice and our own children, it's a good idea to look at the first half of the

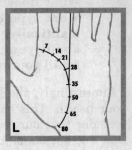

life in detail. For that reason, you will notice the first 35 years have been marked off in groups of seven years each.

● You will find a mark for age seven, 14, 21, 28 and then age 35 on the line. Your eye has to guess the distance in between the marks, allowing ⅐ of the distance for each year between two marks, moving forward one year at a time: seven, to eight, to nine, and so on, until you reach 14.

● Then the next small space represents age 15, then 16, and so on again, till you reach 21. The marked years are guides to help you know just where you are on the life line.

● The years after the 35-year mark are treated differently, and are arranged in three groups of 15 years each. The first set of years includes ages 35-50; the next age 51 until 65; and the last group, age 66 to 80.

● Although the life line is traditionally set up to include 80 years, for years beyond that, the line will extend deeply into the bottom of the hand or wrap around the thumb, indicating the added years.

51

THE HEART LINE

The heart line tells the story of your emotions. Do you respond intensely to others, or are you cool and detached? What does it take to make you happy? What type of person is best for you romantically? Everything you need to know about your emotional life, and how to fulfill your needs, is contained in this line.

Interestingly, the line's color and appearance also reflect your health. This shouldn't be all that surprising when we consider that our feelings affect our health. You could say this line speaks of 'circulation' in a double sense, referring both to the way you extend yourself to others, as well as the health of your circulatory system.

LOCATING THE HEART LINE:
The heart line begins at the outside edge of the hand, under the little finger, and continues across the top of the hand, ending either under the index or middle fingers, or in between them.

BEGINNING PATTERNS:
The heart line should begin in the area of the hand described above. Any exception to this is very rare.

ENDING PATTERNS:
The longest heart line will extend beyond the Jupiter mount, touching the opposite edge of the hand. The typical heart line ends under the Jupiter finger, or in between Jupiter and Saturn. A short heart line will end under the Saturn finger.

PATH ALONG THE PALM:
As it crosses the palm, the heart line is either curved or straight.

As a handy visual aid to determine just how curved or straight the line is, place an object with a straight edge, such as a ruler or a piece of paper, alongside the line.

DEPTH:
As the line crosses the palm, it can lie high or low in the palm, closer to the top of it, or farther down.

INTERPRETING THE PATTERNS

● The longest heart line, extending from the outside edge of the hand and ending beyond the Jupiter mount, reveals great passion. This line means you are intense, and for you, love is all or nothing! Not content with half-measures or games, you openly shower the object of your affection with gifts and attention. In addition, you expect complete devotion in return. (**A**)

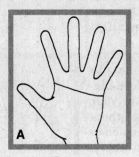
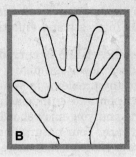

● A long heart line, ending in the middle of the Jupiter mount, means your emotions are lively. You are affectionate and considerate of your loved ones. You live for love, but also understand the give-and-take required for a successful relationship. You ask that your partner truly understand you. (**B**)

● If your heart line ends between the index and middle fingers, you are very realistic in your expectations of love. You understand human nature and are naturally diplomatic, qualities which make for a peaceful home life. This line is a sign of domestic harmony. You are caring and balanced in your affections and get along well with many different types. What's more, you want your loved ones to be happy. (**C**)

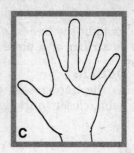

● A heart line that ends under Saturn is considered a short one. This type means that you are not always as patient in love. If you are disappointed in your loved one, you often isolate yourself, turning your attention instead to other matters. After a period of time alone to think things over, you will enter wholeheartedly into the relationship and try again. You crave a wide variety of experiences and you expect your loved ones to support your interests and ambitions. (**D**)

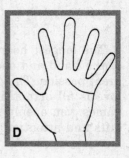

● If your heart line is curved, you are always deep down optimistic, willing to work out any problems in your love life. You are open and enthusiastic in your affections and you enjoy showing others that you care. Your naturally deep emotions are a magnet that attract others. In addition to a lively love life, you find yourself involved in neighborhood or community activities. (**E**)

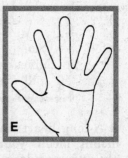

● A straight heart line shows a more reserved nature. This is a person who doesn't easily reveal his feelings. If you have this type of line, you appear cool and detached on the surface, but your feelings may well run deep. It's important to you to make the right decision in love, and you take your time to commit. Because you appear elusive, many people want you. In return, you'd like to be appreciated – but you need your 'space' as well. (**F**)

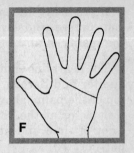

● If your heart line lies high in the hand, order and balance in your life are very important. You like to have your days planned out in advance. This makes you feel more secure and frees your energy to accomplish everything you feel you have to do. You don't like chaotic situations in love and will work to bring understanding and balance into your relationships. You give a great deal to your loved ones because you're dependable and loyal. (**G**)

● A heart line low in the hand indicates a temperament that thrives on excitement and diversity. You see life as a series of new adventures. You find spontaneous fun for yourself and your loved ones. You get pleasure out of the joy and happiness of others. Your feelings often spill over into creative expressions such as poetry, drama, dance and art. (**H**)

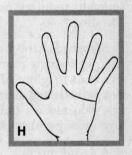

● A heart line ending high on the mount of Jupiter reveals your idealistic nature. You can't always see your loved one's faults, and must make an effort to be realistic in love. (**I**)

● If the heart line ends low on Jupiter, you can see your loved one's faults and the reality of any situation. (**J**)

● The heart line ending high up between Jupiter and Saturn, all the way to the top of the palm, shows a tendency to be jealous, or at the very least a need for a lot of time and attention from your partner. (**K**)

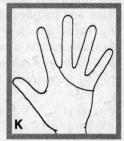

● In contrast, the heart line ending low on Saturn indicates a person who needs to be independent in love. (**L**)

Is your heart line high while your partner's is low? If so, don't think he or she doesn't care. It's just that these two heart lines show two entirely different natures and approaches to love. The relationship requires patience and understanding.

● Sometimes the heart line ends in a fork. This extra 'prong' means you are a dynamo in your affections. You are sympathetic and alert to the needs of others. You always find a way to help in any worthy cause. (**M**)

● A triple prong on the end of the heart line is called the 'humanitarian' line. Early on you get involved in school activities and are drawn to develop your full potential. (**N**)

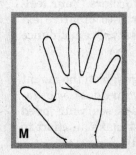

THE HEAD LINE

The head line reveals your determination and momentum in life, as well as the way your mind works. What are your interests? Are you happier with many irons in the fire or do you prefer to concentrate on one special interest? Are you independent? Imaginative? This chapter will show you how to find out.

LOCATING THE HEAD LINE:
The head line begins near the life line, under the index finger, and ends under the ring finger.

BEGINNING PATTERNS:
The head line has five possible variations in the way it begins: Inside the life line/Tied to the life line/Just touches the life line/Slightly separated from the life line/Widely separated from the life line.

ENDING PATTERNS:
The typical head line ends under the ring finger. If it ends under the middle finger, it's considered short, while if the line extends beyond the ring finger, it's long. A very long line ends all the way across the hand.

PATH ALONG THE PALM:
A head line is curved or straight as it crosses the palm. The curve can be measured with the same procedure as the heart line. Occasionally, a head line will have both patterns: The line will typically start out straight in its path and then curve as it crosses the palm.

DEPTH:
A head line can also end high in the palm, near the upper Mars mount or low in the palm, on the Luna mount.

INTERPRETING THE PATTERNS

The way the head line begins shows a person's self-confidence, drive and independence. Confidence is measured by the width of the separation between the beginning of the head line and the life line.

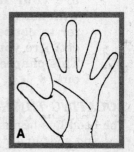

● When the two are widely separated, your confidence is enormous. When the spirit moves you, you feel you can do anything and do it well. You have an uncanny sense of current trends and know just how to position yourself to the best advantage. You are extremely independent and make up your own mind on all issues. (**A**)

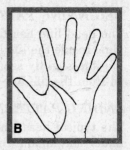

● A slight separation at the beginning of the line shows an equally independent nature, but less need to take risks. You too can build an empire on the strength of your belief in yourself. (**B**)

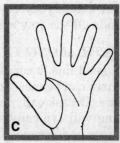

● The head line just touching the life line adds an element of caution to your nature. You'll try anything once you're convinced it is wise or profitable – but only after you have studied all your options. (**C**)

● If the head line is tied to the life line, you are somewhat dependent on the opinion and good will of others as you forge a path in life for yourself. You keep up close family ties and tend to make family of your friends. You appreciate the support of a close-knit group of people. (**D**)

● If the head line begins inside the life line, you are often shy, and need positive feedback from others to feel your best. When life teaches you to toughen up a bit, you can be dynamite. You work hard for the things you believe in. (**E**)

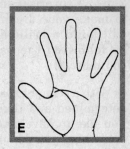

● A short head line means you are a specialist at heart. You latch onto an interest and take it to the max. You should have no trouble rising to the top of your chosen field. (**F**)

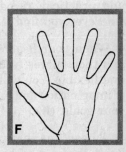

● A long head line ending under the ring finger shows you are interested in a number of subjects and could well succeed at more than one career. (**G**)

● A long head line ending between the ring and little fingers, or directly under the little finger, shows you are enthusiastic about many interests and keep yourself well-informed on a variety of subjects. You like to talk and share what you know. (**H**)

● If your head line goes all the way across the hand to the outer edge, you take life seriously and are driven by a need for achievement. You admire those who have made the most of themselves.

● If your head line is curved, you have a good imagination and delight in life. You love surprises and long for a chance to make your dreams come true. You will build a brilliant life for yourself by following the path that interests you most. (**I**)

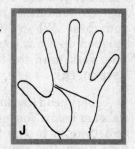

● With a straight head line, you are very determined and take calculated risks. You like to have a solid foundation for everything you do, and you are shrewd and practical, recognizing good value wherever you find it. (**J**)

● When your head line starts straight and then curves, you are both practical and flexible. You will use a combination of imagination and experience to achieve your goals. (**K**)

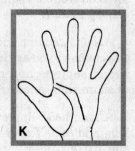

● A head line that remains high in the hand shows good business ability. You can drive a hard bargain if someone presses you. Otherwise, you use your energies to develop the territories that interest you. You are direct in your communication with others. (**L**)

● A head line that dips low in the hand means you make the most of every moment, and you are a romantic.

THE FATE LINE

Behind the glamour of its name, the fate line carries a far deeper and more serious meaning. Actually, calling Saturn's line the 'fate' line gives it a mystique that may be a little misleading. You see, the fate that the line represents isn't something that simply befalls us. Rather, our fate is what we create with our own efforts and responses to challenge and opportunity.

The fate line describes our efforts to grow and adapt to the world as we experience it. It indicates the most advantageous times to respond to opportunities. The strengths or weaknesses in our lives, as well as the choices we make, show up on the fate line.

LOCATING THE FATE LINE:
The fate line is centered under the middle finger and runs in a vertical line from the bottom of the hand to the top of the palm.

BEGINNING PATTERNS:
Interestingly, the fate line has more possible starting points than any other line. Each of the variations indicates exactly how and when we first get our start in life.

If the fate line begins early in the hand, there are three possible starting points: In the center of the palm/Attached to the life line/Slanting from the Luna mount.

If the fate line begins later in the hand, there are five possible starting points: Near the head line/On the head line/Between the head and heart lines/On the heart line/Above the heart line.

ENDING PATTERNS:

Just as the fate line can begin lower or higher in the palm, it can also end lower or higher in the hand. A fate line that ends before the head line is considered 'low', which means the line is short. If it ends above the heart line, the fate line is long. There are five notable endings: Before the head line/On the head line/Between the head and heart lines/On the heart line/Above the heart line.

DEPTH:

Depth here refers to how deeply the line appears to be 'carved' into the hand. As you'll see, a very deep line and a shallow line have contrasting meanings.

PATH ALONG THE PALM:

The fate line is famous for its hard-to-pin-down path in the hand. This line, more than any other, varies in its patterns – both in its beginnings and endings and in the way it crosses the palm.

To further complicate things, the typical fate line is not one line only, but a series of two or more lines, all falling within the track centered under the Saturn mount and finger. This split-up pattern is logical since the fate line shows our shifting fortunes.

⬤ Few people today have a single career from the age of 20 to 70, or the assurance of only one marriage and family. A fate line set up in several sections reflects today's variables in our choices and lifestyles.

⬤ If the fate line is in two sections, these are the two most common patterns: One fate line ends at the head line, and a second line, altered slightly in its course, continues above the head line/One fate line ends at the heart line, and a second line, altered slightly in its course, continues above the heart line.

⬤ Most palms have a number of vertical lines. There is a

62

rule to help you know which lines are fate lines: The fate line alone is connected to the Saturn mount. Any other vertical line is not a fate line.

INTERPRETING THE PATTERNS

BEGINNING PATTERNS: When your fate line begins in the center of the palm, you are very independent by nature and appreciate best the success that you alone create. (**A**)

● If your fate line starts attached to the life line, the support and influence of your family helps you make your way in life. (**B**)

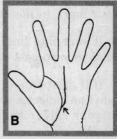

● When your fate line begins on the Luna, you will have the support of friends and mentors to help you get ahead. (**C**)

These three beginnings to the fate line reveal how you will make your way in the world. The next step is to understand when you will start on your path, prepare for a career and prepare for adult life. The fate line begins at the time you get your start in life.

For some people, this start comes early, perhaps as young as age 10 if they make a decision that later results in a career. In this case, the fate line begins right at the bottom of the hand.

The more typical fate line begins later, higher up in the palm. Here are the meanings for five variations:

● If your fate line starts just below the head line, you will be in your late 20s when you get set in a career and establish your adult life. (**D**)

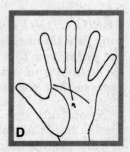

● If your fate line starts exactly on the head line, you have your first success at age 30. (**E**)

● A fate line that starts between the head and heart lines shows you make your mark in life at age 35. (**F**)

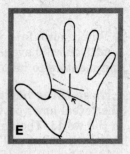

● If your fate line starts on the heart line, your success comes at age 40. (**G**)

● If it starts above the heart line, the fate line indicates you establish yourself in your career and lifestyle after age 40. (**H**)

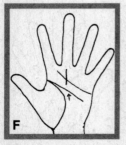

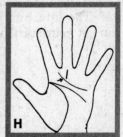

NOTE: If your fate line starts at the points described on the previous page, the meaning is not understood in the same way as that of the earlier discussion of fate lines. Rather than say you literally just establish yourself at or after a certain age, these lines indicate that you don't recognize your success or have the sense you have done your best until this time in your life.

ENDING PATTERNS: The fate line's ending signals the end of your major efforts to develop your career and lifestyle. After the line fades, you no longer make a push. You can rest on your success or expand what you have already developed. In a way, the time when the fate line ends can be thought of as going on 'automatic pilot'.

● Ending before the head line, your fate line reveals that you made your major efforts in your 20s, and must have been a boy or girl wonder. Now you're sitting pretty! (I)

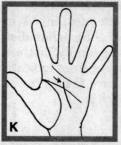

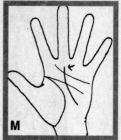

● If your fate line ends right at the head line, you are well established by the age of 30. (**J**)

● A fate line ending between the head and heart lines speaks well of your mid-30s as the time you realize your ambitions. (**K**)

● If your fate line stops right at the heart line, this shows solid success at age 40. (**L**)

● A fate line that ends after the heart line shows a long career path – years of effort that culminate in the fulfillment of your expectations after age 40. (**M**)

DEPTH: A deep fate line strongly engraved in the palm shows the periods of our greatest successes. Very few fate lines have the same depth as they go from the bottom to the top of the hand, because not every year in our lives is equally good or productive.

● A shallow fate line, appearing to be only lightly traced on the palm, shows years of uncertainty or indecision. But as long as the line is there, you are making progress, even if you have stress or doubts about your life.

PATH ALONG THE PALM: A fate line in two different sections means either a change of career or a change of direction within the field you have already chosen. Your attitude and goals will change, due to experience and circumstances you meet in your day-to-day working life.

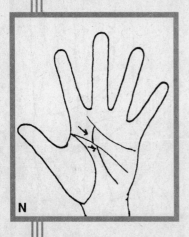

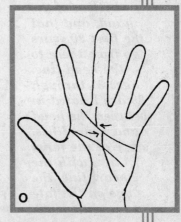

● If your fate line ends at the head line and starts again after the head line, you will experience this change at age 30. (**N**)

● If the fate line switches course at the heart line, then you will experience your goal changes at age 40. (**O**)

TIME ON THE FATE LINE: *In a palm reading, timing is everything. In addition to the life line, the fate line is set up to mark the years in a life. You may have already realized that, since most of the fate line's meanings on the previous pages involved the concept of time.*

● When we make something of ourselves – and what that something is – is represented in the diagram below: (**P**)

Notice that time on the fate line begins at the bottom of the hand, and that the first 30 years go from there to the head line. Ages 31 through 39 are located in between the head and heart lines, since at the juncture with the heart line, the age on the fate line is 40.

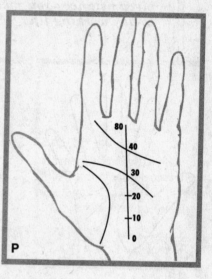

You will see that ages 41 through 80 are in the fairly small space between the heart line and the very top of the palm. This may look strange, especially when you note that the first 30 years are spread out over half the palm.

But think about this for a moment. When you are young, time seems to go slowly, especially when you're a child waiting for Christmas, a birthday or school to get out. As you get near 40, time takes on an entirely different aspect. At which age did you stop counting the days till your birthday? When did time start to fly by so fast?

The small space allowed for the years 40 through 80 is a psychologically accurate portrayal of time.

Once the points on the fate line for the years 30, 40 and 80 are established, it's possible to divide these segments in sections to visualize the other years in a life span.

The first 30 years are divided into three equal sections of 10 years each; ages 31-39 are found within the space between the head and heart lines, and each year is 1/10th of the space. The last 40 years are divided into four sections of 10 years each.

Practice will get you comfortable enough to gauge the years by eye and make your calculations accurately. Start by taking the halfway point between the major 'marker' years, and work up or down from there.

As an example, to locate age 35, look at the point exactly halfway between the head and heart lines. To find age 60, do the same between the heart line and the top of the palm. To find age 45, picture first one quarter of the entire space, which is age 50, and then take half of that to reach age 45. (**Q**)

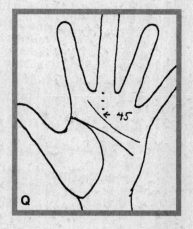

You know the good years in a life by locating the deepest part of the fate line and fixing the time according to this procedure. Or, if you want to be prepared for challenges in your efforts to succeed, find the weaker aspect of your fate line, time it, and take precautions to prevent or overcome the challenges that might arise.

The ability to 'tell time' in the hand is the real test of a palmistry pro. Once you have mastered this technique, your readings will be more fun and satisfying. You will certainly get people's attention with this skill!

PALMISTRY,

The Secrets thereof

DISCLOSED,

Or a *Familiar Easy*, and *New*
Method, whereby to *Judge* of the
most *General* Accidents of Mans *Life*
From the *Lines* of the Hand, withal its
Dimensions and Significations.

Also many Perticulars added, Dis-
covering the *Safety* and *Danger* of
Women in *Child-bed.*
VVith some choice *Observations* of *Phisiognomy*,
and the *Moles* of the Body.

As also that *Most Useful Piece* of *Astro-
logy* (long since promised) concerning
ELECTIONS for every *Particular* Occa-
sion, now *Plainly* Manifested from *Ratio-
nal Principles* of ART.

The Second Time Imprinted.

And much Inlarged by the Author,
RICHARD SAUNDERS,
Author of the Former Book of *Chyro-
mancy* and *Phisiognomy.*

*Cuiq; sua est tempestas, & tempus cuique voluntati
sub Cælis*, Eccle. Cap. 3. verse 1. to 12.
Tempus est potentius Legibus.

LONDON,
Printed by H. Brugis for G. Sawbridge, at the Sign
of the Bible upon Ludgate Hill, 1664.

THE APOLLO LINE

The Apollo line points to something special about a person, to an extra dimension to the personality. Here you find charm, warmth, spontaneity, cheerfulness, creativity and great expansion in your life.

Finding someone with a good Apollo line is like having permanent sunshine in your life. The line speaks most of talent and personality, and for that reason has often been taken to mean 'fame'. Perhaps recognition is a better word. A good Apollo line gives charisma and entry into a charmed circle of friends who share the same interests and talents.

LOCATING THE APOLLO LINE:
The Apollo line is a vertical line centered under the ring finger.

BEGINNING PATTERNS:
Like the fate line, Apollo can begin high or low in the hand, but rarely does it begin at the bottom of the hand. If Apollo does start low in the hand and continues up beyond the heart line, it is considered 'short'.

There are five variations to the beginnings of Apollo: Below the head line/On the head line/Between the head and heart lines/On the heart line/Above the heart line.

ENDING PATTERNS:
Most Apollo lines end above the heart line, while many exist only in the space above the heart line, making this space the ending point as well.

PATH ALONG THE PALM:
The Apollo line should be straight. It rarely curves in from

Luna, but occasionally the line can appear to waver as it travels up the hand.

The line doesn't shift at the head or heart lines like the fate line, but two or three Apollo lines might be found in a hand, above the heart line. Any definite line above the heart line, centered under the ring finger, is an Apollo line.

DEPTH:
The Apollo line can be deeply engraved on the palm or traced faintly on the surface of the hand.

INTERPRETING THE PATTERNS

● With a long Apollo line, you are often the apple of other people's eyes. Long used to being the center of attention, you strive to live up to people's expectations of you, and you genuinely enjoy life. The more unusual and interesting your routine, the better – for you are very creative and express yourself well. You can go straight to the top – and perhaps even be found in Who's Who. (**A**)

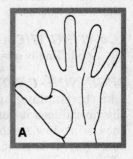

● If your Apollo line is short, you find satisfaction in leisure activities that reflect your personality and creativity. Hobbies pay off, and you find you can easily expand any opportunity you are given. You are often asked for advice and could surely become someone's mentor, especially in the arts, theater, literature or the media. (**B**)

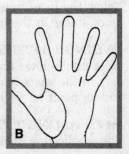

● An Apollo line beginning below the head line means that early on, people placed their bets on you. Perhaps you were a cheerleader, football hero or valedictorian. You continue to shine in your adult years. You love music and everything beautiful. (**C**)

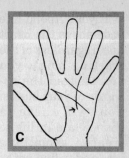

● When your Apollo line starts at the head line, you are well on your way to success by 30. If the line continues on above the heart line, and beyond, your track record won't fail you. You back up one accomplishment with another. (**D**)

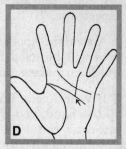

● With an Apollo line starting between the head and heart lines, you have enough serenity, wisdom and experience by age 35 to know who you are and what you are going to create in this life. (**E**)

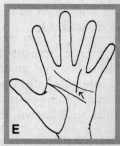

● If your Apollo line starts on the heart line, you know you have worked hard and gained enough knowledge to do something extra in life. You can expand in business and take up writing or a career in communications. You come across as an expert. (**F**)

● An Apollo line starting above the heart line means you will find moments of great satisfaction later in life with plenty of time to dream and plan leisure activities or travel. (**G**)

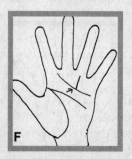

73

● If your Apollo line ends above the heart line, regardless of the starting point, you are assured the rewards of your labors. You will have a chance late in life to create something new and to find adventure where you least expected it. (**H**)

● A straight Apollo line means your talents will be used to their fullest. You will have success and recognition. (**I**)

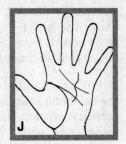

● If your Apollo line is wavy as it goes up the hand, you will have success, but you can't count on it at all times. Circumstances sometimes get out of control, but with a bit of effort you can continue to do well. (**J**)

● Two or three distinct Apollo lines above the heart line mean you have a variety of interests, all of which could make you a little plumper in the pocketbook or else quite well-known. (**K**)

● A deep Apollo line (A) brings the most success into your life, as well as adventure and happiness. (**L**)

● A faint line (B) .has its merits, too. You will find yourself led to fortunate opportunities by a set of co-incidences in life. (**M**)

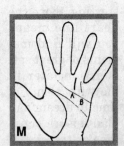

THE MERCURY LINE

The Mercury line means business! Although small in comparison to the size of the other lines, it's a sure anchor to success. If it's deeply carved into the palm, it reflects a sound body, an unworried mind and a flair for the business of life. When the line is straight and solid, on the other hand, the senses are sharpened and the instincts are good.

Life can fall into place quickly for anyone who has a strong Mercury line. These people have the blessing of feeling very much alive, of wanting to have the best life offers, and of possessing the wit to go after it.

LOCATING THE MERCURY LINE:

This line lies at an angle in the hand, starting near the bottom of the life line, continuing across the hand in a diagonal direction and ending under the Mercury finger.

BEGINNING PATTERNS:

The Mercury line starts: Near the bottom of the life line/Attached to the life line/In the center of the palm, half an inch or so away from the life line.

ENDING PATTERNS:

The longest Mercury line ends right on the Mercury mount. A shorter line ends between the head and heart lines. The shortest line ends before the head line.

PATH ALONG THE PALM:
A Mercury line can be either straight or wavy in its path. In addition, a line may be solid or broken into two pieces. Occasionally, a Mercury line will be only a series of lines, resembling dashes, as they cross the palm.

DEPTH:
The Mercury line can be deeply carved into the palm or lightly traced on its surface.

CRESCENT:
Occasionally, a Mercury line will be shaped like a crescent and sit at an angle similar to that of the fate and Apollo lines.

INTERPRETING THE PATTERNS

● Starting near the life line, your Mercury line means you have good instincts and a flair for recognizing sound value in real estate or other purchases. You are good in sales or in any profession where others need to believe in you and your services. (**A**)

● Attached to the life line at its start, your Mercury line indicates you will use the early part of your experience as a background to help you launch your own business. You may be halfway through one career before you feel the pressure to change and acquire your own venture. (**B**)

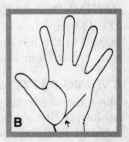

● Starting about one-half inch away from the life line, the Mercury line means you love to be informed about business and to keep abreast of financial trends. You are most likely interested in the stock market and other investments. (**C**)

● With a long Mercury line, your business ability is tops, and the prospect of having your own business is irresistible. Many people with this line become consultants in order to have a variety of outlets for their flair for business. You are happiest when you are on the move, spending time and money well. (**D**)

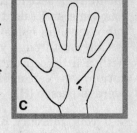

● If your Mercury line is short, you're certainly in the running when it comes to financial and business ability. Watch and learn from others and you will find an appropriate outlet for your business talents. Your health is good, your nerves strong. Challenges are no problem. (**E**)

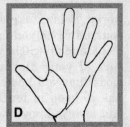

● A straight Mercury line means you know your way in the world. Little fools you, as you are alert and very motivated to be a success. All the business ability a good Mercury line indicates is yours, as is the business area of your choosing. Happy hunting! (**F**)

● A wavy Mercury line indicates your occasional need for advice and reassurance as you pick your way through a multitude of confusing options in business. Yes, business is tricky. But have courage; you're up to it! (**G**)

● A solid Mercury line is the surest sign of the shortest route to success. Nearly everything you put your hand to will turn out to your satisfaction because you use your time and talent effectively. A solid, unbroken line holds a message of benefits for you through your sound instincts. With a little concentration and determination, you can achieve more than the average person.(**H**)

● If your Mercury line appears as little dashes, you have a tendency to fret and worry. Relax, take a deep breath, center yourself when you face a challenging moment, and all will be well. You need to take care of your diet and eat more of the foods that you know agree with you. You like to keep in touch with many friends and always know the latest news. (**I**)

● When your Mercury line appears in two sections, the meaning is similar to the fate line that switches paths at the head or heart line – it signals a change in the direction of your business interests. You profit by being alert to changing trends in the marketplace. (**J**)

● A strong Mercury line is the surest sign of success, especially in business. When the line is also deep, you can look forward to good health and prosperity.

● When the Mercury line is shaped like a crescent, this is a special sign of intuitive ability. You can play your hunches and succeed. Listen to your inner radar. Yoga and hypnotherapy are two areas of study you would enjoy. (**K**)

78

SPECIAL FEATURES

By learning how to analyze the lines' beginnings, endings and the path they take along the palm, we've completed the first step toward a full understanding of them. The second step is to consider any marks or variations they may have.

The marks most often found on a line are a square, bar line, cross and dot.

SQUARE: A square signifies protection, offsetting any weakness in a line. Problems will be avoided or cleared up easily. A square is very desirable because it helps guard against other, more serious conditions represented by the rest of the marks.

BAR: A bar line shows a brief problem or obstacle.

CROSS: This mark reveals a more challenging problem or condition represented by the last three marks.

DOT: This is a sign of tension.

These meanings affect the message of the particular line on which they appear. Remember we talked about telling time on the lines? At what age the marks appear will help the person do some advance planning for impending problems.

VARIATIONS IN THE LINES' APPEARANCE:

The most frequent variations in a line's appearance are: Breaks, islands, chains and forks. Of these four, only a fork increases the line's strength. The others represent a general weakening of the force of the line or else a change in your life's direction.

BREAK: *A break interrupts the flow of a line and normally shows a change of direction in the area of life the line represents.*

● **HEART LINE:** New outlook on love

● **HEAD LINE:** New interests or career

● **LIFE LINE:** Lifestyle change

ISLAND: *This variation refers to a period of particularly low energy as well as a feeling of restriction and confinement.*

● **HEART LINE:** Frustration and depression or discouragement

● **HEAD LINE:** Overall fuzzy thinking and tough decision-making

● **LIFE LINE:** A period of lower physical energy

CHAIN: *Chains on a line 'muddy the waters' and show a period of confusion. When a chain appears on a line, pursuing any goal that adds to a sense of stability and security helps steady the influence of that line.*

FORK: *This is a definite plus. The added segment or extra prong strengthens the line.*

● **HEART LINE:** More ability to love and more emotional satisfaction in life

● **HEAD LINE:** Talent and clear thinking

● **LIFE LINE:** Possibility of two residences, perhaps a city home and a country home

RELATIONSHIP & CHILDREN LINES

Everyone is interested in the question of marriage and children. The hands speak on this issue, but popular notions of what they can show are loaded with misconceptions. Thinking that one line means only one marriage, or that two guarantee two marriages, is too simple a view.

Everyday experience working with these lines will show the true dimension of their message. They speak of the heart's wishes. The human heart is complex, and love too complicated an issue to be described strictly from a 'numbers-game' point of view.

To analyze these lines accurately, we must be aware of what they can and cannot reveal. They do not necessarily describe the number of marriages or children in exact detail. They show the desire for a relationship or children, the ability to be a good partner or parent, as well as the best time to be in a relationship or to bear children.

The 'marriage' lines are better called 'relationship' lines because the hand doesn't talk in terms of legal realities. As we know, not every marriage line means a trip to the altar. Any deep line in the relationship area of the hand shows the potential for a rewarding union with another person.

RELATIONSHIP (MARRIAGE) LINES: Like all small lines on the palm, relationship lines (A) can change. They grow stronger and deeper when the time for a relationship approaches. When the timing is off or desire absent, they appear weaker and faintly traced on the hand. (**A**)

Because the lines can change, and especially because a person can change, we have to be careful about using these lines as indicators of different unions with different people.

Here are guidelines to a better understanding of these lines:

● A strong, clear relationship line means a desire for a deep, meaningful association. Real love is possible, and a union is indicated.

● A deep line is a sign of commitment.

● Occasionally, there are no lines in this area of the hand. This doesn't literally mean there will be no marriage. If lines are absent, then the person simply doesn't put a lot of himself into a relationship. He or she has a 'take it or leave it' attitude about romance.

● More than one line in the relationship or marriage area speaks of growing happiness or contentment in marriage or a close relationship with the same person. However, if a person is divorced or single, then second and third lines are a sure sign there will be another meaningful relationship.

● When a strong line grows fainter, this is a sign the person is not satisfied with the relationship or with marriage, and steps need to be taken to ensure that the current relationship continues. It may be time to assess the relationship, to find out why it's not working, or how it could improve.

CHILDREN LINES: These lines (B) present a special challenge to their interpreter. They don't often represent the actual number of children a person has, or will have, but rather, they show an interest in or affection for children. To have children lines in your hand is a sure sign you want children. But will you have them?

● To determine this, look at all the lines. There are usually several, but a few of them will stand out because they are deeper and straighter than the others. These lines may be used to predict children.

● There may be one strong line, or two or three. In any of these cases, children are likely to be a part of your life. The deep lines almost always represent biological children. Occasionally, these deep lines refer to stepchildren, especially if you have a particularly strong relationship with them.

● Children lines talk about parenting ability. If you have even one line, you can be a good parent or stepparent. Two lines increase both your skills as a parent and your enjoyment of children. Teachers often have deep children lines, referring not only to their own children, but to their students, especially if they relate well to them.

● To understand what the palm has to say about children, concentrate on the clearest and strongest of the lines. Then you be the judge. Do you see two outstanding lines? That indicates two children. Now ask yourself: Do you want two children? That's for you to decide first. The rest is left to fate.

TIMING THE RELATIONSHIP LINES

Time as expressed by the relationship lines can be very accurate. It's a good guide to an upcoming relationship, as well as to the best times to put energy and effort into developing that union.

To determine timing, look at the outside edge of your hand. The relationship area starts at the heart line and goes up to the little finger's base. Divide the area into thirds, with two marks. (**A**)

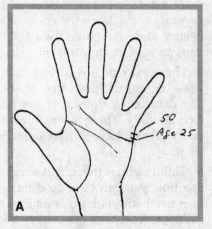

The first mark represents age 25, and the second, age 50. Any line closer to the heart line than one-third up that area means a relationship earlier than age 25. The years 26-49 fall in between the two marks, and with practice, you will be able to establish approximate years, perhaps learning to spot age 30, 35, 40, and so on, and then fine-tuning the process until you can see 31, 32, and on up to the 50th year. Any line after the 50-year mark predicts a relationship for 51 forward. You should learn to divide that section too, to answer the question of 'when' a relationship will happen.

INTERPRETING THE PATTERNS

A strong, deep relationship line promises you great affection and a lasting relationship, or one that greatly alters your life, giving you many valuable lessons.

A weak, thin relationship line means you don't let love rule your life. You will not have the highs and lows that romance brings because you are reluctant to reveal yourself to another person or to take the chance of complete surrender.

A weak line followed by a stronger one means you are growing in your ability to commit to a relationship and to be content in one.

Two or three relationship lines show you will have a lifetime of romantic liaisons. You are made for relationships.

● A relationship line that ends with a fork shows a tendency to have a relationship that doesn't last, for any number of reasons. This is called the 'divorce' line in many books, but just think of it as indicating challenging moments in love, not a guaranteed divorce. (**B**)

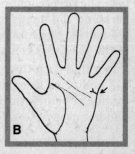

● If the relationship line has an island on it, there will be periods of separation, because one or the other partner wants it, or perhaps because of career demands and travel. (**C**)

● A broken relationship line foretells periods of stress in a relationship, but with care and work, it may well survive.

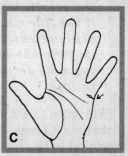

85

THE HANDS SPEAK

We all have questions about our lives. Sometimes they're big ones, for which there is no easy answer. If we were to ask someone about a probable outcome for our biggest concerns, we would most likely meet with silence or an admission of "I don't know."

It is at these times that the hands can be of interest – and of help! Their message, seen through the lines, shape, size, and all the features we have just learned to analyze, can help us...or at the very least distract us! To have a way to face our preoccupations, to stretch our minds a little, to understand the hands' message, all this can be a relief. And to lessen the pressure, even just a little, through the guidance of the hands, is a blessing.

Working with the hands over a period of time will give you the ability to use them as a tool for understanding the potential in your future. But for now, let's look at the answers hands can give to a few of life's more burning questions.

LOVE: "Am I ready to be married?" Yes, if the relationship line is deep and clear, and if the fate line is strong. If the Apollo line is also present, this is a sure clue to happiness in your choice. A curved heart line, sweeping wide across the hand, predicts fulfillment in love.

"Will it last?" Yes, if the relationship line is long and straight. If there is a break in the line, or an island or fork, there is a possibility the relationship won't last. A line which slants slightly upward means difficult moments will arise, but patience and understanding can help.

> **HEALTH: "Am I healthy?" Yes, if all the lines are solid, with no breaks or islands or chains. The deeper the lines, the greater the potential for good health, because these lines show a sound body and strong constitution.**

If the lines have islands, you might see a nutritionist to make your diet the best for your personal needs, including boosting your energy. If the head line has a chain on it, near the beginning, you could use a multimineral supplement.

"Am I physically fit?" This question is of great interest today. Any hand that is firm to the touch, elastic feeling, and not soft, means you are physically fit. An even color on the palm's surface adds to your general fitness.

> **MONEY: "Can I make money?" Yes, with a combination of several or all of these signs, you will succeed: a long, strong index finger, a very straight fate line in the center of the hand, a thick middle finger, or thick fingers in general, a thick base to the palm, a long thumb, or a long tip on the thumb.**

These are definite clues to the ability to generate income. If your ring finger is long, you are a risk-taker. And if your hand has a selection of the traits above, you will surely win at the gamble you take in business.

"Can I manage my money well?" Now that you've made your money, what will you do with it? If your head line turns up toward the Mercury mount, or if your head line is very straight, you will invest it. If your head line is curved, you will want to keep a part of your earnings for pleasure.

If your fingertips are square, or your Saturn mount large, you will head to your savings account at the nearest bank. If your nails are square too, you have a natural ability to hang on to your money and make it work for you.

● "Will I inherit money?" An inheritance or a grant is very likely if you have a good Apollo line, or if you have two parallel lines, one on either side of your fate line. It is a 'legacy' pattern. (**A**)

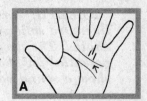

● "Will I be financially secure when I am old?" Yes, if you have a very tiny but important line. A line between the middle and ring fingers, at the top of the palm, shows security in your later years. You will be comfortable. (**B**)

> *CAREER AND TALENT: The hands provide a good guide to the work we would enjoy most because it is the work we can do well.*

The following are a few key traits for selected talents:

WRITING: You have writing ability when you have a large Mercury mount, or a large Luna mount, or this special sign: a head line which ends in a long fork with the bottom prong extended into the Luna mount.

TEACHING: You are a natural teacher if your Jupiter and Mercury mounts are well-developed. A special aptitude for teaching is also indicated by a square on the Jupiter mount.

ACTING: This is your field if you have a spatulate tip on your ring finger, a good curve on Upper Mars, and a wide space between your thumb and hand when you extend your thumb.

LAW: This career calls to you if you have the classic sign of a small, well-balanced fork at the end of your head line, with both prongs of the fork equal in size.

ACCOUNTING: Anyone with a well-developed Saturn mount, a long Saturn finger with a square tip and a square nail would excel in this field. A straight head line is also a plus.

BUSINESS: You will do well in business if you have a wide base to your hand, large Venus and Luna mounts, a long thumb, and spatulate fingertips.

MARKETING: Marketing talent is indicated by a head line separated from the life line at its start.

COMMUNICATIONS: This field appeals to you if you have a high Mercury mount, a curved head line, and a fate line that curves in from the Luna mount at its start. An Apollo line is another plus factor.

ENTREPRENEUR: Entrepreneurs have thick hands, wide nails, which are often spatulate-shaped, and a deep head line with a slight curve on it that is separated from the life line.

SERVICES: All human resources fields appeal to you if your Luna is long and well-developed, if Venus is high, your head line has a slight curve to it and your fingertips are round.

MEDICINE AND PSYCHIATRY: Success in these fields comes with a large Mercury mount, three vertical lines on the Mercury mount, a large Jupiter, a head line that just touches the life line and a long thumb. Thick hands are an asset for a surgeon or physician and thin hands have a more analytical turn of mind and are suitable for psychiatrists.

MANAGERS: Good managers in any field have round hands, a well-developed Mercury mount, and short fingers.

REMEMBER: With the scope of the hands' information, your future need not remain a total mystery. You create it as you respond to life and make your choices. Palmistry is meant to be a gift of added insight to help you shape yourself and your future to a standard of excellence that brings you satisfaction and success – and luck!

FINGERPRINTS

It's no mystery why for more than a century crimefighters have dusted for fingerprints in their quest for suspects. Like snowflakes, the mysterious markings on your fingers are absolutely unique. And, writes palmist Carol Williams of Dallas, Texas, in this fascinating bonus chapter, they reveal hidden abilities and traits every bit as important as those found in the palms.

ARCH   LOOP   WHORL   TENTED ARCH   DOUBLE LOOP   PEACOCK WHORL

QUALITY: The quality of the lines on the fingertip is the first clue to the overall personality.

STRONG, clear lines indicate a person with a practical personality. They like action and results. They appreciate the material world and use their hands and body to accomplish tangible goals. Sports stars, craftsmen, and managers often have these strong lines.

FINE, easily visible lines that are crossed by many other tiny lines going in different directions denote a born salesman or actress. Their need for adventure, enthusiasm for life, and love of people keep their lives a constant whirl of action. So what if they're a little egocentric and always want to be in control? With them life is never boring!

LIGHT fingerprint lines that can easily be seen with good light or in direct sunlight indicate an organizer and a love of communication. Investigative reporting, journalism or marketing are the perfect careers for these light-lined people. Add a dash of curiosity and a love for beauty and you have a top-notch private detective or real estate agent. Just don't get too upset when their love of detail leads them to organize your private diaries according to the Dewey Decimal System!

If the fingertips appear to have no lines at all, or lines that are just barely visible even in strong light, you're dealing with an idealist. These are highly sensitive people. High ideals and a belief that things should be perfect are the basis for their constant striving to make the world a better place. As environmentalists, healers and religious leaders, they often make considerable differences in the world around us.

PATTERNS: Once you've noticed the quality of the fingerprints, look closely at the various fingers and note the patterns on each one. There are three basic types of fingerprints: the arch, the loop and the whorl. Don't expect a hand to have only one type of pattern, because there's usually a mixture. You many find an arch on one finger, a whorl on one, and loops on all the others.

THE ARCH is a simple raising of the parallel fingertip lines to form a hump in the middle.

Arches are usually located on the index finger and on hands where the lines are clearly visible. These people are practical and down-to-earth. They are ambitious and probably believe that money brings happiness. If the arch is seen on the ring finger, you'll impress the person with the largest diamond ring you can afford because they have a natural love for jewelry. Arches on the thumb are rare, but if they exist, watch out for rebellion, especially in the teenage years.

As 'arch' people age, they tend to revert back to the traditions and beliefs of their childhood. They feel a need to test authority yet again. Once they've found the rules or a 'guru' that work for them, they defend them at all costs. Don't expect to change their religion or their values system.

● Those with arches on the index finger work well in team situations and with groups. Watch out for their emotions, however. Arch people, especially those with 'tented' arches (where the hump is taller and a small triangle appears under it), tend to ignore their emotions and emotional situations. The tented arch is the sign of the emotional volcano, especially when found on the index finger. These 'volcanoes' seem calm and peaceful, hiding their emotions from themselves and others until one day they simply erupt.

● Men and women of action have arches on the middle finger. Don't give them a book about how to do something – show them. They learn best by doing. You'll hear a lot about the 'school of hard knocks' and how valuable it is from this type.

● When you find an arch on the ring finger, look for a wedding ring there, too. Traditional family values are important to these folks. Most 'arch' people will seek out marriage and family to fulfill their inner need for security and love.

● If you go for the silent type, look for an arched print on the little finger. You'll have to pry information out of this one, because they'd rather show you than tell you. On the flip side, if they do talk, it will either be a constant stream of gossipy chatter, or talk about anything except their true feelings.

● If by chance you find arches on all the fingers, you probably have a revolutionary on your hands, quite literally. In this case, action, not words, wins out in every area of life. This person will fight against everything and everybody to have his own way. The word 'stubborn' comes to mind when dealing with these individuals. On the positive side, give this person a job on a football team, or make them a part of a political campaign they believe in, and they'll rise to the top.

THE LOOP is characterized by the swooping of the lines up from the crease of the finger to form a loop directed toward the thumb or little finger. There is usually a small triangle formed by the lines near the crease area where the parallel lines  *are divided from those forming the loop.*

This is the most common fingerprint type. Adaptable, 'go with the flow' types usually have loops on their fingertips. They strive for balance in all aspects of life.

● Lawyers, diplomats and trade negotiators tend to have loops on their thumbs. They look at both sides and bring balance to a situation. People with looped thumbs often find themselves listening to their friends' problems and giving helpful advice.

● If a loop is on the little finger as well, you might as well become a psychologist and get paid for it because you're already doing it for free! If you have a double loop, be careful because you may have 'too much of a good thing'. You have a tendency to see too many sides of a situation and consequently not be able to make a decision. If you do make up your mind, it may be too late. The double loop is good for dealing with lots of details though, and is often found on the hands of CPAs, librarians, analysts and corporate lawyers.

● Loops on the index finger show an ability to work in many situations under many types of management. You get along well with all kinds of people. Promotions usually come through recognition of work well done, not through a need to push yourself to the top.

● You're open to new ideas when you have a loop on the middle finger. You have a 'live and let live' attitude toward others – that is, until they try to force you to conform to their standards. Listening to their viewpoints is fine with you, but you'll make up your own mind later. If you have a double loop on this finger, philosophy and religion appeal to you. You'll investigate these fields and enjoy debating the various ideas.

● A comfortable home, harmonious, peaceful surroundings and nature are all important to those with a loop on the ring finger. If the print lines are strong, gardening and construction careers as well as any area dealing with the environment and the outdoors are good choices. If the lines are faint or invisible, hire a maid.

● Loops on the little finger are found on healthcare professionals, journalists and technical writers. The easier the lines are to see, the more the person is inclined to talk. Conversation and communication are important and cover a broad range of subjects. Dealing with feelings and an inborn need to help others are further characteristics of the little finger loop.

● A loop that starts from the little finger side and points toward the thumb is called an *ulnar loop* and is the most common. If the loop starts from the thumb side and loops toward the little finger, however, it's a *radial loop*, which is much rarer. If this Radial Loop is found on the index finger, it's a sure sign of success and a unique outlook on life. This person will be outstanding in some way.

THE WHORL, the most complex pattern, is also the easiest to spot. The lines form a circular pattern on the fingertip and two tiny triangles are visible near the parallel lines next to the crease.

The whorl pattern is not as common as the loop and the arch. It's found mostly on the ring and little fingers. Creativity, individuality and egotism are indicated by the whorl. These folks love to try new things and ideas.

● If there are whorls on all the fingers (a rare occurrence), this person is probably a law unto himself. Dictators, fashion designers and rock stars are all likely to have whorls on most of their fingers. Their anger may flare up suddenly, but it dies out just as quickly. Extravagance can cause financial problems unless the whorl person's uniqueness pays off. This is the sign of the extremely rich and the extremely poor because whorls indicate risk-takers. If their individuality and creativity are put to good use, they can become overnight successes. On the other hand, if their uniqueness is not recognized and appreciated, they find it very difficult to fit into other people's molds.

● When the whorl is found on the thumb, the person is determined and able to get things done. They conquer obstacles or at the very least use them to their best advantage. Bossiness and a need to control can be a problem for fellow workers. Watch out for these.

● Go into business for yourself if you have a whorl on your index finger. It's the sign of success in the career of your choice (if you control your desire for constant change). You need complete control of your working hours and the way the job is done. Work for others only if they give you the freedom to do things your own way.

● Researchers, trivia collectors and archaeologists have whorls on their middle fingers. Seeking out new and ancient knowledge of all kinds is essential to their happiness. Their ultimate goal is to build new theories based on this knowledge. Research scientists looking for new cures and Indiana Jones-types have this whorl in common.

● Whorls on the ring finger are the sign of the successful artist, entertainer or dancer. This is also the sign of the romantic lover. Charm and versatility are the order of the day, and they'll keep you constantly entertained. If whorls are present on many of the other fingers though, you'll have to be constantly surprising them, or they may be unfaithful. It's not that they don't love you – they just love variety, too.

● Whorls on the little finger show distinction in the broadcasting field or in medicine. If you have a whorl here, you're a good talker. But if the entire little finger is long, beware of your tendency to lie, because you do tell a good story.

● If whorls appear both on the ring finger and the little finger, become a novelist or scriptwriter. Creative stories flow out of you and you probably live in a fantasy world. This is especially true if the lines are faint.

● A slight tail coming out of the circle in the middle of the whorl is called a Peacock pattern. This is extremely rare and the sign of creative genius. Talent may cover many fields, however, and the person may skip from one project to the next before seeing results from the first one. Addictions may be a problem for this person as an escape from the practicality of the real world. If a Peacock person can be organized and motivated by someone practical, however, they can offer the world great innovations and new creative expressions.

> *STRAIGHT LINES: You may see additional straight lines running horizontally across the fingertips. These are found on all the fingerprint types and are signs of procrastination. How long and deep they are indicates just how much you like to put things off. These lines appear most often on the thumb. If you see them on all the fingers except the thumb, you'll finish most things on time.*

● The opposite is true, however, if you see the lines only on the thumb. If the lines are on the thumb and all the fingers, you're not only a procrastinator, but also a worrywart. Ulcers may be in your future!

After looking at several sets of fingerprints, you'll notice that most people have a healthy mix of pattern types. Learn what each pattern means on a particular finger and eventually you'll see how they all interact to give you a clear picture of that person's character traits. Reading fingerprints allows you to learn things about yourself and others that you hadn't noticed before. It can also be a tool to help you know and use your own strong points and to recognize and eliminate problem areas. Most of all, it's fun!

THE END